The CAT'S

Library of Congress Cataloging-in-Publication Data:
Seuss, Dr. The cat's quizzer: are you smarter than the cat in the hat? / by Dr. Seuss.
p. cm..
SUMMARY: The cat in the hat plays quizmaster by challenging the reader with both entertaining and educational questions such as "Are freckles catching?" and "How old do you have to be to drive a car?"
ISBN: 0-394-83296-5 (trade)
1. Questions and answers—Juvenile literature. [1. Questions and answers] I. Title
GV1507.Q5S454 1993 031.02—dc20 92-17409

Manufactured in the United States of America 31

QUIZZER

By

Dr. Seuss

Beginner Books
A Division of Random House

The ANSWERS
(if you need them)
start on page 58.

Here is
Ziggy Zozzfozzel with his sister Zizzy.
They got 100%.
They got every question WRONG.

Are YOU
smarter than
a
Zozzfozzel?

Which end
of a bee
stings you?

Do elephants
have uncles?

2

Which Grows Faster?

An uncle's eyebrows . . . ?
Or an uncle's mustache?

Are there
a few ducks
on the moon?

Are FRECKLES catching?

Where do
peanut trees
grow?

China . . . ?
Japan . . . ?
U.S.A. . . . ?
Where else . . . ?

Aww... those
are too EASY!
On we go to
something HARDER!

Now...

Look at this picture.
Look at it hard.

6

Then turn the page . . . .

QUIZ

about the page before.

How many wheels
on the Cat's wagon

Was there a
flag on the house

Was the Cat
holding his umbrella

Did the big
yellow animal
have blue dots

If YOU
owned the big
yellow animal, what
would you call it

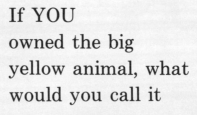

9

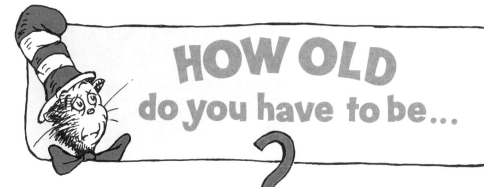

HOW OLD
do you have to be...

?

... to be a Boy Scout?

... to be a Girl Scout?

... to drive a car?

... to fry
an egg?

10

. . . to vote for President?

. . . to BE the President?

And . . .

How old
do you have to be
to be a Japanese?

How Long
can you play
Stare-Eyes
without
blinking

?

How Long

can you play
STARE-EYES
without
laughing

?

Which can go HIGHER?

A Bee?

An Eagle?

A Balloon? . . .

14

. . . . Or someone
with a Helicopter Cap?

TRUE OR

Only redheads
can wiggle their ears.

A camel
never drinks water
on Thursdays.

FALSE?

A cat is always
shorter than his shadow.

Your shadow is
always longer than you are.

There are more
doughnut holes
in the world
than doughnuts.

17

Who will go

Joe . . . ?

Higher?

Or Moe?

19

A NIGHT

Do horses sleep standing up?

Do roosters sleep on their backs
. . . or on their sides?

Do fish sleep
with one eye open?

QUIZZER

There are
FLASH-LIGHTS
for when it's dark.

Are there
FLASH-DARKS
for when it's light?

Which turtle will get to
the Pizza Palace first?

23

LAVA
comes out
of a
WHAT?

WHAT comes out
of a WHAT?

WHAT
comes out
of a
TREE?

24

WHO
comes
out
of
a
WHAT?

WHAT is it that comes
out of a WHAT-IS-IT?

TONGUE QUIZZER

How fast can you say . . . ?

Ellie's Elegant Elephant
Ellie's Elegant Elephant
Ellie's Elegant Elephant
Ellie's Elegant Elephant
Ellie's Elegant Elephant
Ellie's Elegant Elephant
Ellie's Elegant Elephant
Ellie's Elegant Elephant
Ellie's Elegant Elephant
Ellie's Elegant Elephant
Ellie's Elegant Elephant
Ellie's Elegant Elephant
Ellie's Elegant Elephant
Ellie's Elegant Elephant
Ellie's Elegant Elephant
Ellie's Elegant Elephant
Ellie's Elegant Elephant
Ellie's Elegant Elephant
Ellie's Elegant Elephant
Ellie's Elegant Elephant
Ellie's Elegant Elephant
Ellie's Elegant Elephant
Ellie's Elegant Elephant
Ellie's Elegant Elephant
Ellie's Elegant Elephant
Ellie's Elegant Elephant
Ellie's Elegant Elephant
Ellie's Elegant Elephant
Ellie's Elegant Elephant

FOOD

Do the Japanese
eat with
pogo sticks
or joss sticks?

Does spaghetti grow on land
or under water?

QUIZ

What do Italians call macaroni?

Do pineapples grow on pine trees or apple trees?

Tell me three things YOU had for dinner last night.

AND...

Can
YOU
do
this
easy trick?

WHO WILL WIN?

The X's
or
the O's?

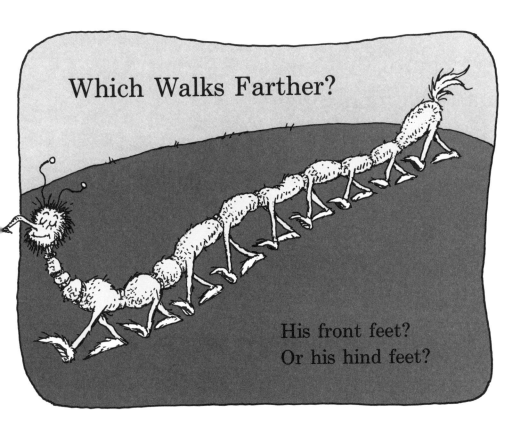

Which Walks Farther?

His front feet?
Or his hind feet?

Would you rather
have more QUESTIONS
or
would you rather
have the MUMPS?

Me? I'd rather have the MUMPS.

31

Are there
many women kings?

Are there
any women uncles?

AND...

33

If a dinosaur
walked into
your back yard . . .

. . . what is
the first thing
you would do?

In Ireland, you can buy rainbows.

THAT
is
Zizzy Zozzfozzel.

FALSE?

Snails are faster than turtles.

It is not safe
to ride backwards
on an ostrich.

What

would you do
if
you
sprouted
a
Daisy?

Would you run
and see your dentist?

Would you water it
and grow more of them
and sell them
to your friends?

Or would you try
to grow some roses?
They're worth a lot more.

Which goes Farther...

A Ping-Pong Ball
or a Bow?

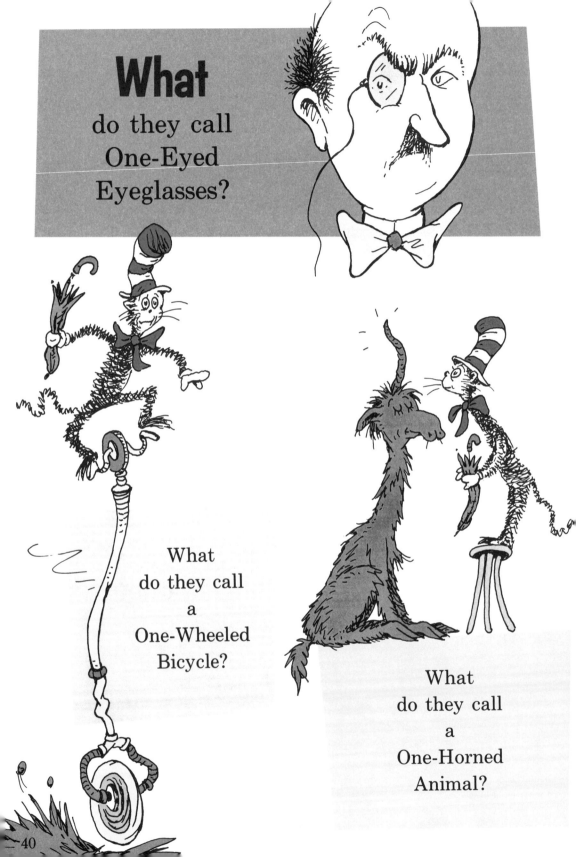

What

do they call
One-Eyed
Eyeglasses?

What
do they call
a
One-Wheeled
Bicycle?

What
do they call
a
One-Horned
Animal?

WHAT

would you do
if you jumped in the air
and you didn't come down?

This <u>could</u> happen, you know.
So you'd better
have an answer.

Here are four WHAT?

Are you
upside down in a spoon?

What is
your
Zip Code?

This wheel
goes
this way.

That makes
this wheel
go
this way.

Please tell me!

Am I going
Frontwards
or
Backwards?

43

It's getting **HARDER** and I'm getting **TIRED.**

Everyone's tired. But we **MUST GO ON!**

Are there more
A's or Z's
in the alphabet?

Where do crows
hide soccer balls?

44

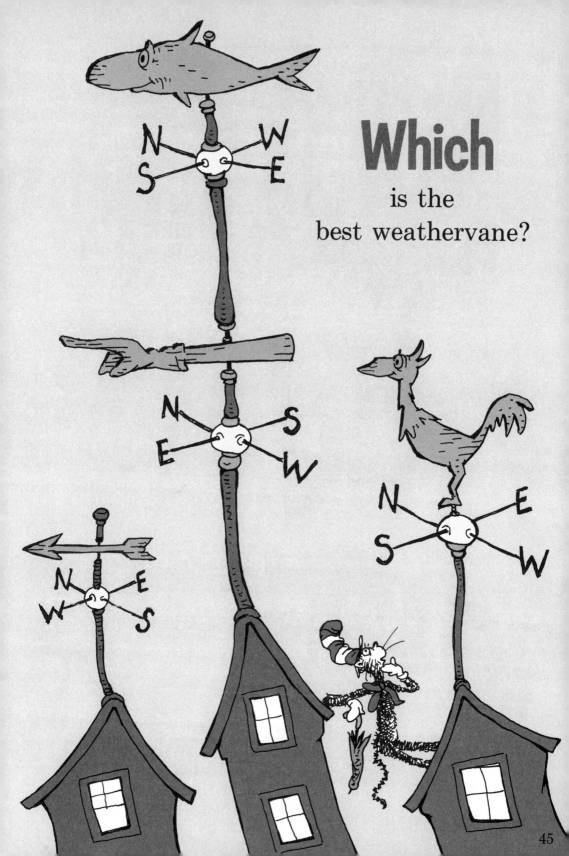

Which
is the
best weathervane?

What was George Washington's favorite TV program?

Do worms dream?

Does Joe
look closer to Moe
than Moe looks to Joe?

Who
will get
the
banana?

47

WHO
will get
the MOST BANANAS?

What was
ABRAHAM LINCOLN'S
middle name?

WHO WILL LOSE?

The X's
or
the O's?

Does your family have
a one- or two-car grudge?

50

WHERE would
you go to learn
to play the
stethoscope?

In Yosemite Park . . .

. . . do
the bears
take photographs?

Are you
OLDER
than
your teeth?

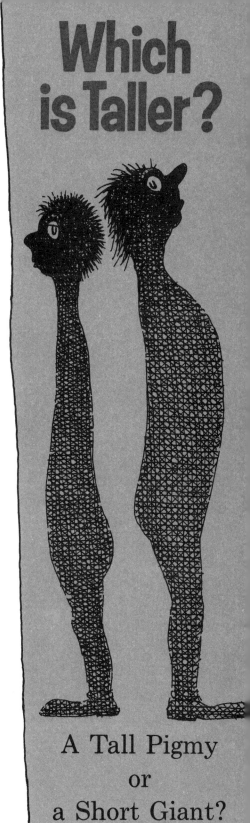

Which is Taller?

A Tall Pigmy
or
a Short Giant?

Here are more than 100 things
that begin with H.

(The Zozzfozzels could find only 6.)

The ANSWERS

PAGES

2 and 3

A bee's stinger is in back. You're safe up front.

Most elephants have uncles. And aunts. And cousins, too.

Your uncle may not know it, but his MUSTACHE grows faster.

4 and 5

No ducks on the moon. (No elephants, either.)

Dr. Robert Bernstein, the freckle specialist, says, "Don't worry. You can't catch them."

There are <u>no</u> peanut TREES. Peanuts grow under ground. Like potatoes.

8

ONE WHEEL on the wagon.

Yes. A FLAG on the house.

The UMBRELLA is on a hook.

<u>No</u> BLUE DOTS on the animal.

If it's a boy animal, I'd call him Augustus. If it's a girl, I'd call her Gertrude. But <u>you</u> don't have to.

10 and 11

Boy Scout: You can be a Cub Scout at age 8. A regular Scout when you are 11.
Girl Scout: You can be a Brownie at age 6. A Cadette at age 12.

To drive a car in most states you have to be 16.

To fry an egg . . . ? Go ask your mother.

You can VOTE for President when you are 18.

You can BE the President when you are 35.

All Japanese are Japanese the minute they are born.

58

12 and 13

STARE-EYES
My cousin Joe can do it for an hour,
but he says it hurts his feet.

14 and 15

An EAGLE goes higher than a bee.

A BALLOON goes higher than an eagle.

But nobody goes anywhere in a Helicopter Cap.

16 and 17

Ear wiggle: False (My uncle can do it and his hair is black.)

Camel drinking: False (Camels don't like to be thirsty on Thursday.)

Both shadows: False (It all depends on how high the sun is.)

False—if you count jelly doughnuts.

18 and 19

JOE will go higher.

20 and 21

Some horses do. Some horses don't.

Roosters don't sleep on their sides or backs or their stomachs either. They sleep on their feet.

Fish sleep with both eyes open. (Poor fish. They have no eyelids to shut.)

I never heard of a FLASH-DARK, but I'd sure like to have one.

22 and 23

The RED TURTLE will get there first . . .
if he goes through the first hole to his left.

24 and 25

LAVA out of VOLCANO.

SAP out of TREE.

CUCKOO out of CUCKOO CLOCK.

JACK out of JACK-IN-THE-BOX.

And everybody knows that a WHATSIS comes out of a WHAT-IS-IT.

26 and 27

You can say "Ellie's Elegant Elephant"
as fast as you like—but not to me.

28 and 29

Pogo sticks they jump on.
Joss sticks they burn.
They eat with CHOP STICKS.

Spaghetti doesn't grow. It's made out of flour and other stuff.

What do Italians call macaroni?
They call macaroni MACARONI.

Pineapples grow on pineapple bushes.

I don't know what they gave you for dinner. All they gave me was Cat in the Hat food.

30 and 31

It's an easy trick . . . if you have six fingers.

The O's should win. They have the next turn.

His front feet and his hind feet and his middle feet all walk the same distance.

Speaking of MUMPS . . . can you say it backwards?

32 and 33

No women kings. Only women queens.

No women uncles. Only women aunts.

34 and 35

I've always wanted to go to Alaska.
That's what I'll do when the dinosaur comes.

36 and 37

Buy a rainbow: False (They're too hard to wrap up and take home.)

Zozzfozzel: False
(That is ZIGGY. Not Zizzy.)

Snails: False
(Snails can go only 3 inches a minute. They could never win in a turtle race.)

Ostrich: True
(You couldn't catch me riding backwards on one of those things.)

38 and 39

Sorry, I can't help you. It's your daisy. Not mine.

A PING-PONG BALL goes farther.

A BOW doesn't go anywhere.

40 and 41

One-Eyed Glasses: MONOCLE

One-Wheeled Bike: UNICYCLE

One-Horned Animal: UNICORN

If you get stuck in the air, fly to the nearest telephone. Dial "0" and ask for a ladder.

42 and 43

Here are four what? Four PALMS, of course.

Everyone, even a cat, is upside down in a spoon.

BACKWARDS!

I'm sorry, but I don't know your zip code. Mine is 92037.

44 and 45

Only one A and one Z in the alphabet. (But there are 5 Z's in Zozzfozzel.)

This is the only good one.

Crows hide keys and money and bottle tops. But SOCCER BALLS? Never!

On all the other weather vanes, North, South, West and East are placed wrong.

46 and 47

There was no TV in 1776. But George did pretty well without it.

I know two famous psychiatrists— Dr. Willis and Dr. Mazzanti. They tell me that maybe worms DO DREAM.

The little monkey will get the banana!

Joe looks closer to Moe than Moe looks to Joe.

48 and 49

Dog will get only one banana. Cat will get no bananas at all.

Ask your doctor where he learned to play his stethoscope.

The bears in Yosemite Park tell me that they never take photographs.

50 and 51

Abe Lincoln had no middle name. But he did pretty well without it.

The X's WILL LOSE—if the "O" guy doesn't goof.

A GRUDGE is not a GARAGE. If you think it is, you need a lesson in spelling.

You are older than your teeth. But you are the same age as your left big toe.

I know that a short pigmy is never taller than a tall giant. And a tall giant is never shorter than a short pigmy.

But about the tall pigmy and the short giant—I give up on that one.

The 100 H's

13 <u>Hot</u> dogs
1 <u>Hen</u>
5 <u>Hail</u> stones

1 Camel <u>Hump</u>
1 Garden <u>Hose</u>
2 <u>Hinges</u>

1 <u>Hockey</u> puck

4 Clock <u>Hands</u>
1 <u>Hair</u> on
1 <u>Hairbrush</u>
24 People <u>Hands</u>
1 Worm <u>Hole</u>

1 <u>Hundred</u>
2 <u>Helmets</u>

1 <u>Halloween</u> pumpkin
  hanging from
1 <u>Hole</u>

1 <u>Hockey</u> player

1 <u>Hot</u> candle
1 Pair of <u>Hot</u> Levis
1 <u>Heel</u> on shoe
1 <u>Hoola Hoop</u>

1 <u>House</u>
7 <u>Hearts</u>
2 Animal <u>Horns</u>
1 Blowing <u>Horn</u>
1 <u>Hockey</u> stick
4 <u>Hats</u>

4 <u>Hooks</u>
  (One for Fish)
1 <u>Hoe</u>
1 <u>Ho</u>
1 <u>Hoo</u>
1 <u>Hedgehog</u> eating
1 Panty <u>Hose</u>

2 <u>H's</u>
1 <u>Handbag</u>
1 <u>Hammer</u>
1 <u>Ham</u>
1 <u>Handkerchief</u>

2 <u>Hockey</u> skates
1 <u>Hatchet</u>

1 <u>Horse</u>
6 <u>Hoofs</u>
3 <u>Horse</u> shoes
1 Pair of <u>Handcuffs</u>
1 <u>Hair</u> ribbon

1 <u>Hippopotamus</u> in
1 <u>Hammock</u>

1 <u>Hoot</u> owl <u>Hooting</u>

1 Umbrella <u>Handle</u>
  and
15 other <u>Handles</u>

1 Mystery man
  in a <u>Hood</u>

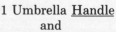

and
1 Cat

with a <u>Headache</u>!

Dr. Seuss

. . . said that he had a hard time finding someone who would pay any attention to his first children's book. Happily, that never happened again . . . that book and the more than forty-two others he wrote since have all become modern classics.

The most famous of them all may be *The Cat in the Hat*. This extraordinary story was so revolutionary in its impact that it created a new kind of publishing for children: Beginner Books, books that children could read (and delight in) all by themselves. With the Cat as their symbol, and Ted Geisel (as Dr. Seuss was known when he wasn't writing or drawing) as their editor, Beginner Books and Bright and Early Books have helped millions of children discover what great fun reading can be.